To Ash T   ieR

Strategic Parenting for the 21ˢᵗ Century: Not my Enemy

Keep Shining :)

Sandra D. Johnson, MHSC

Love you Sandra John #BonusMom ♡

This is the first book in a series on the topic of Strategic Parenting by Sandra D. Johnson of @MadiselCoach and The Madisel Group, LLC.

Scripture quotations marked NLT are taken from the New Living Translation of the Bible, copyrighted 1996, 2004,2015. Used with permission.

Scripture quotations marked ESV are taken from the English Standard Version of the Bible, copyrighted 2001, 2007, 2011, 2016. Used with permission.

All definitions found in dictionary.com or Merriam-Webster, founded in 1831. Used with permission.

DEDICATION

To all the teenagers, parents, and staff members that I
have had the privilege to work with and serve since 1998.
My life has been greatly impacted through the
interactions and challenges that we learned and faced
together. Thank you for your willingness to learn and
experience life with me through the stress of change,
struggle, and transition.

Learning new things and growing into maturity is not
easy and can take more time than we sometimes want.
But it will always be worth it. My life is better because
you entered it. Thank you for choosing life as we
journeyed together.

CONTENTS

ACKNOWLEDGMENTS

I am grateful to the many who encouraged me to put my thoughts on paper and share with whomever will listen. Specifically, much appreciation goes to Crystal A. Johnson & Myhosi "Josie" Ashton for being fellow child advocates and life facilitators. Thank you for always setting the bar high when serving others. I enjoyed making a difference together.

Thank you to my family (all my sisters and brothers) and friends who shared many parenting stories for the life journey. An extended thankfulness goes to these mothers who gave me some extra experience at one level or another: Sylvia Johnson, Heather Komondoreas, Ashley James, Ashley Fenn, Emily Hargrove, and Laura Fane. You ladies are beautiful mothers and warriors.

Great appreciation for the encouragement from the proofreaders, fellow authors, and accountability partners: LaRonda Howard, C Jai Graham, Alvin King, Paige Cummins, Mary Johnson, Vanessa Jefferson, Stephanie Tatum, & Kesha Gordon.

Finally, I am forever grateful to the late Robert Sr. and Ida Mae Johnson, for being the best Grandparents to me and my siblings.

Introduction

What does identification and parenting have in common? Both can be demanding and confusing in this culture. Identification will always be an interesting topic for humans. Maybe it is because, identification brings us a sense of belonging and acceptance on many levels. Therefore, let me open this book by identifying myself as an ***unparent***. This misspelling is presented here on purpose. I chose the word because when typed into a message or note on a digital device, the auto correct says "I parent" or "No replacement found". I champion both of those descriptions.

My personal definition for an *unparent*, is a person who works with children, studies the behaviors of children, advocates for the needs of children, and learns from children while in the context of never having the privilege of holding the official title of parent, as defined in the culture. The *unparent* does grunt work: they babysit, teach, coach, train, support, advocate, protect, correct, lead, love and encourage children everywhere. This *unparent* has invested over 25 years of service to become a resource and subject matter expert on children and youth. I do not believe that anyone is required to experience childbirth or the adoption process, to gain empathy and awareness for what a parent will experience in the journey.

There is nothing simple about parenting. The position of parenting is often misunderstood and criticized by those with and without the title. It is the only job that is continually described as having no manual to know how to properly conduct self.

Furthermore, it is one of the most demanding positions that impacts and influences future leaders all over the world. The past is the past and what is done is done. But if there is a better way—a strategy, should we consider it? Let's define the word strategy. Merriam-Webster's dictionary defines strategy as a careful plan or method. The idea of being careful means that one is intentional about what they are doing.

The word ***strategy*** is a simple word but the situation requiring a strategy can be very complex. Parents, will you consider partnering with me as we discuss some strategic methods for being intentional with parenting the next generation?

What does it mean to be a strategic parent in the 21ˢᵗ century? If you are reading this book, your curiosity will answer that question. We become intentional by creating a strategy for our thoughts and behaviors for parenting young people. Thank you for making yourself available to engage in the process.

*Special Note to my readers: *This book is for parents at any age and stage. The concepts are mainly focused in on dealing with pre-teens and teens. If you wait until they get to that age, you will have missed the preparation years. Take your time with these thoughts and suggestions. It might seem overwhelming at times, but please stay the course. The thing about parenting, even if the situation does not fit you, there will be a neighbor or coworker whom you can help. Therefore, have a journal ready to take notes and reframe my words and thoughts* *to work for your situation. There is no perfect fix to family dynamics and parenting struggles, but you may find some helpful techniques to add to what you are already preparing and doing. Some of this new thinking might be difficult to digest. Please stay encouraged and do what works well for your family. I honor you with this work.*

"Strategy is a careful plan or method."

Chapter 1: The Engagement Concept for Parenting

When you consider how you interact with your children, what obstacles and issues do you encounter? One of the saddest phrases that I have heard coming from teenagers or parents is when one says, "I want nothing to do with that person!" This phrase is usually stated due to some form of emotional or physical hurt that has happened in the relationship. As a coach and counselor for family restoration, it is very challenging to talk about restoring relationships when one party does not want to interact with the other person.

When we have any form of interaction or connection with another person, it fits into the category of engagement. Do you have any rules or guidelines for how you will engage or connect with your children? Let me encourage you to not just leave this up to chance. It is important to have a strategy for interacting and creating connections. The military has given us some great information when it comes to interacting with others, especially in difficult situations. As your child gets older, there is bound to be more opposition in the relationship.

The military has a concept called Rules of Engagement (ROE). The idea is that a military authority has set some guidelines and boundaries for how to engage in combat. Sometimes in the family relationship the smallest misunderstanding can erupt into an oppositional battle. These oppositional battles can also be called power struggles. For example, here are a few questions that start small but can escalate very quickly. Who moved my headphones? Why are the dishes not washed and put away? Did you clean your room? Who touched my stuff? Why is the Wi-Fi password not working for me?

The purpose of this resource is to encourage adults to become more strategic in their parenting of this generation of young people. With this resource, we desire that parents identify that children and family dynamics are not the enemy. We each must accept that there are many attacks from an enemy (or multiple enemies) towards the idea and purpose of family.

We will give you some ideas, concepts, and strategies to challenge the traditional views and to upgrade the status quo of parenting. A strategy is designed to challenge how one thinks. Engagement is about being present and aware of what is going on. Here are some basic ingredients for engagement to assist with parenting in the 21st century. These ideas will be developed more in other chapters.

1. **Lay aside the failures and amplify the successes.** Take the time to look for things that are going well with your young person. The older they are, the more aware they are of their own personal failures. Try not to constantly remind them of their short comings. Make it a habit of finding and identifying areas of strengths and positive change in attitudes and behaviors. Let them know that you noticed. Please continue to be their biggest supporter, even when things are difficult. Your strength is a great example for them.

2. **Encourage Engagement.** Create a welcoming environment for your young person to be enticed to join in. Family should be where we learn about unity, not several independent and disconnected parts. Some simple areas of engagement are chores, cooking, planning, and creating things to do as a family. Welcome your young person to plan meals and activities for the family. A key

hindrance to engagement and the lack of motivation for today's youth is criticism and judgment from adults! The parent must also be an active participant. Make sure you are engaged as well, not just working all the time. All device time must be managed and not allowed to hold any member of the family hostage.

3. **Look beyond the performance of good grades or the lack thereof.** What do you know or see in your young person about their creativity and character? Hard work and follow-through on assignments is a great goal and a wonderful teacher. Please remember that children are still developing physically and emotionally. Children need to play and have fun, which includes being silly and loud. Children learn through discovery, therefore, do not crush or stifle their creativity and exploration. Giving your best does not always equate to earning an A+. What character traits are being discussed and developed in your young person? What type of person are they becoming?

4. **Parents need real rest and relaxation whenever possible.** Put rest on the schedule if that's what it takes to make it a priority. Do not allow the fact that you have too much to do to become your

escape from taking care of yourself and well-being. Is it possible that you have too much to do because you have not delegated enough to members of the family? Everyone, who is able, must help in the family. When everything depends on the adults, the children will have an unhealthy view of family and working together to accomplish greatness. Exhaustion can produce hostility. Hostility is a closed door for deeper relationships and an open door for anger and anxiety to fester. Also note, getting rest can also include seeking counseling or coaching for your unresolved personal issues. You are a valuable member of the family. Rest well while you are alive.

5. **Get on the welcome list!** Your young person (especially between the ages of 10–18 years old) has an unwritten list of people, places, things, and ideals that are welcome in their world or mind. If you watch and listen carefully, you might learn who is on the list and why they are on the list.

- Ask for an invitation.
- Don't demand or bully your way into the relationship.
- Don't always threaten to shut down Wi-Fi and take devices. (This is a precious resource, therefore use it strategically).

Ask yourself: Why do I want to be on the welcome list? Your number one reason must be **RELATIONSHIP!**

If you get on the welcome list, ask about the rules. Remember, you do not have the right to be on the welcome list. Treat it like a privilege.

Honor and respect the rule maker, even if the rules are not to your liking. Also note, the rules and requirements for being on the list might fluctuate depending on the age and gender of the young person. Do not assume that because you got on the list when your child was 11, that you are still welcome when they are 13. Stay aware and just re-apply.

6. **Respect your child.** Respect is a gift. The meaning and concept of respect is highly misunderstood and misused. This is mainly because we place limits on the idea of respect and we only highlight it when we feel we are not on the receiving in of what is owed to us. Parents and adults are the first examples of what respect looks like in the relationship. Consider what kind of example that you have been in this area. Stop waiting to receive respect and just give respect to the younger humans in your care. Because we have been trained to believe that we have the right to be respected, we have lost sight of the privilege of being respectful to our children.

   Being a parent is a privilege, not a right. If the parent is not cultivating a relationship with the young person, then do not expect or demand to be respected. The relationship is a prerequisite for respect, not the other way around. Respect does not create relationship. Respect strengthens a relationship.

All the above points are just bite-size pieces of topics for engagement. You can create your own check off list of the six items mentioned above to start your strategic parenting journey. Use the list for self-evaluation, accountability, and improvement.

Consider this:

Pause and ponder the helpful thoughts provided in this chapter. What did you hear for the first time? What can you put into action over the next three weeks? Remember that you have a powerful position of influence, everything counts.

"**Respect does not create relationship. Respect strengthens a relationship.**"

Chapter 2: Expect More

Times have really changed. This is a new era and technology keeps everyone guessing about the newest upgrade in the next 30 days. Once we get the latest device or upgrade, we test it out to see what improvements have been made. We generally expect more of technology and indirectly expect less from the younger generation. Is it possible that we have been pacified to believe that young people cannot accomplish great things until they are adults? Adults say things to young people like: "When you get older, you will understand" or "wait until you have kids, you will see what I'm talking about". I propose that this is an upgrade generation, therefore we should expect more of them.

Being older in age does not guarantee any deeper understanding of life issues. Furthermore, some people will never have the privilege of parenting children. All of this is about teaching our children how to accept, understand, and demonstrate empathy. So, the "wait until you grow up" statement can easily become an escape from the needed conversation. Resist the use of the phrase so that you keep the door of communication open.

Teach **empathy** to your children. Empathy means the ability to understand and share the feelings of another. Now that we know the definition, show them what empathy looks like in real time. Teenagers engage in empathy very easy, listen at how they will explain and defend the behaviors of peers, celebrities, or social media connections. By the way, this is a great place to start teaching and discussing more about the topic of empathy. Feel free to use the examples and peer interactions that your young person gives you. Furthermore, expect them to show empathy in your home without arguing with them or demanding it. Talk about empathy, ask about empathy, and share your own stories and behaviors of empathy with your young people.

When **responsibility** is taught and expected, young people transition into maturity of thoughts and actions. Make room for them to rise to the occasion. Parents should be the first adult to see and identify mature behavior in your young person. Expect a conversation with them that does not involve a device. If texting incomplete words and emojis are the depth of conversation in your family, then it is unlikely that anyone will advance to mature conversations. The younger, developing minds will retreat and possibly avoid future interactions with healthy communication skills.

Being a teenager is not a phase that we get over. They are becoming the type of adult that they will be, right now. Teach them to own that character and to adjust now, not when they grow up. Some people never "grow up" or demonstrate mature thinking. *The tween & teen years are simply years of transition into adulthood*. It is the human version of the metamorphosis of the caterpillar's transformation into the butterfly. Expect change, challenge, and confusion, but talk more about personal character and expect more in their character development. Make room for them to grow and develop into emotionally healthy adults.

Every stage of life is the transition into what is next. Some of the relational struggles that happen, during the teenage years, is in direct response to low expectations or uncommunicated expectations. Telling this beautiful, developing mind to only "make good grades" is base. Some parents will even add "stay out of trouble", which is thrown in for good measure. This could be interpreted as: pay someone to do your schoolwork and just don't get caught.

Expect more of them and re-evaluate what you mean and what a young person hears and how they interpret what the parent says. Remember that this is the "upgrade generation" and they expect more, therefore, parents should expect more also.

Consider this: Don't just say: "I expect you to go to college". The young people of this generation need higher expectations that are rich with character. Raise the standard by including statements of completion. Here is an example: "I expect you to graduate from college in a program of study that you enjoy". This statement has lifted the conversation to a higher level of thinking. This statement is loaded with characteristics that require goal setting, follow-through, loyalty, commitment, self-worth, obedience, and determination. We all want all these things and more for our children, but we make statements of expectations that are void of these qualities.

"Every stage of life is the transition into what is next."

Chapter 3: Misguided Control

Join me as we listen in on a classic scene of "The Parent & Teenager Conversation".

Situation: The teenager has been restricted from phone privileges and parent is ready to negotiate reinstatement of phone-life happiness and "world peace" in this home.

Youth: "Mom, can we talk about my phone now?"

Parent: "Yes, you have done well during this restriction, so I am looking forward to returning the phone to you".

Youth: "Well, here's what I think…I spoke to the service provider via video chat and they said I need an upgrade, so I think we should just go to the store and change out this phone for a better quality phone that will function better with the latest system upgrade"

Parent: "No! We are not doing that, I just spent $900 on back to school clothes and shoes and now you want me to care about the latest phone upgrade created by a billion-dollar company?" "No way!! Not happening."

Youth: "You are so unfair! You can't even let me explain! You never listen to me. I hate our relationship!"

Parent: "Okay, well, since you hate me, I'll just hold on to your phone for another week for your ungrateful and disrespectful attitude."

Youth: "Fine! I DON'T CARE—You Can have it!!" Walks away, slams two doors and says: "I hate this bull crap! I can't wait to be out of here".

What just happened? What do you think needs to be repaired in this relationship?

Let's get our *Strategic Parenting* sights and sounds in tune. This is a classic example of the use of viewing each other as the enemy, therefore a combat style of response is communicated.

The least obvious is the most important: **The fight for control**. Not control of the situation or circumstances, but control of the other person. It appears that the teenager wants control of the parent, which then means control of parental decisions. The parent wants control of the teenager, which then means control of household peace.

Both angles for control are wrong. This is misguided control. The key control feature that is missing, in this scenario, is self-control. Each person would highly benefit by controlling the natural response of over-reacting to the other person.

No one in this scenario is exercising their original capacity for self-control. The teenager needs self-control to accept an answer of "no" and not fall apart. The parent needs self-control to help guide the young person to stay on track, as well as, not allowing the young person's reaction to create personal hurt feelings.

"I am not your enemy."

The next item to resolve is **the concept of focus**: keep the main thing the main thing. The priority for the young person was to regain the phone, old or new. As time went by without a phone, the young person was continuing to devise a plan. The young person had a vision for a better phone, which only comes through upgrades. *The young person adjusted the priority without notifying the parent. This is very common with young people in the 21st century.* When we know how our family (team) members think, we will work better together.

Parents, please pay close attention here: The young person demonstrated great thinking by *working on what is next*, instead of complaining about *what is negative now*. The young person had a good idea for improving the overall situation, it was just presented at the wrong time.

The young person has created a great opportunity for teaching and re-enforcing some wonderful character traits. These character traits: tenacity, negotiation, conversion, initiative, and creativity arc the exact skills that any hiring manager would enjoy. But the parent failed to notice the skill and therefore could not re-enforce the skills by talking to the young person about the poor timing of the incident.

Young people, by their growing nature, will create many scenarios for adults to teach healthy character traits. Unfortunately, when youth feel belittled or judged by the responding adult, the opportunities for teaching and learning healthy character traits decreases.

As we further examine the response of the parent, please allow me to slip into some language of football. The comments from the adult produced a few fouls. Here the referee would throw several yellow flags on the field of play.

First, the parent missed a huge opportunity to affirm the young person by recognizing the idea as a good one. The young person exercised an engaged mind in thinking of a product improvement. We live in a time of constant change and improvements. The children of the 21st century have only known a world of upgrades. Think about it, upgrades are happening all the time for these digital items that we all depend on. We must meet and interact with young people in that world of upgrades. In other words, they think and process life issues through an emotional system of immediate change and improvements. Because this topic demands more time and space, we will deal with it later in the series. The world of technological improvements is not an enemy of the family. Consider what upgrade the family relationship might need.

Second, the parent has forgotten that they gave the young person a compliment by saying that the youth had done well during the restriction. This must be considered when the irritation in the conversation causes one to forget. The youth had already served their restriction; therefore, the phone should not be continually held because the restriction was successfully served and lifted. The additional restriction of the phone will now rightfully be considered as unfair, which creates more power struggles in the relationship.

In addition, the parent needed to get more information before shooting down the ideas presented by the teenager. This could be accomplished by asking questions instead of getting into feelings and complaining about how much money was spent on back to school.

Here is an alternative strategy for communication:

Parent: "I see that you have been researching some alternatives. What motivated you to get more information about a new phone? Can we get this upgrade without paying any additional fees? What is the deadline for making this upgrade?" These questions can help avoid a power struggle and opposition by creating an atmosphere where the young person feels like they are being heard. This is a great opportunity for your young person to learn about negotiation, firsthand. Furthermore, it keeps the door of the relationship open.

Consider this: These relationship landmines can be very damaging to the family connection. This is especially true when things are mishandled and misunderstood. To avoid these types of power struggles and misguided control, **consider pausing and asking questions before shutting down the youths' idea for some type of improvement**. Feel free to tell us some alternative strategy that you have used that helps the relationship. Send your email responses to info@themadiselgroup.com

"Consider what upgrade the family relationship might need."

Chapter 4: Structure—Punishment, Discipline, & Consequences

Let's talk about structure and organization in our homes in the 21ˢᵗ century. Everyone is very busy and trying to accomplish something great personally and collectively. What type of structure does your house operate in? What type of order or organization do you have? Mealtime schedules. Bedtime routine. Chores. Shopping. Taking care of pets. Bill pay patterns. School time schedule. Work time process. Play time focus. Whatever answer you give to these topics will provide insight on how you handle discipline, punishment, and consequences in the home.

We may not be aware that a lack of structure and order in

the regular, daily life routines, can communicate that behavioral matters are met with the same lack of structure and chaos.

Children who are raised without structure and discipline have safety and security issues that create a lack of personal and emotional stability. The lack of stability can encourage issues of anxiety and undue emotional and mental stress. Please take time to consider this issue and evaluate your position on the topic.

What is the difference between discipline and punishment? Let's first explore punishment and its origin. From dictionary.com, the word **punish** means:

1. to subject to pain, loss, confinement, death, etc., as a penalty for some offense, transgression, or fault: *to punish a criminal.*

2. to inflict a penalty for (an offense, fault, etc.): *to punish theft.*

3. to handle severely or roughly, as in a fight.

4. to put to painful exertion, as a horse in racing.

I included most of the example definitions so that we can

see that we use them all at different degrees. These definitions are powerful and helpful in understanding how we interact with our children. Over the passing of time, punishment has become a threat of violence and harm. I have heard many parents proclaim that they will *"beat the hell out"* of their children for several infractions. The key thing to remember here is the power of words. Please be aware of the implications and confusion that these type statements cause.

It is said that **punishment** can be based on fear and control in the relationship with the person in authority. The fear factor of the relationship is rooted in the desire to raise or groom a "perfect" child who is a model citizen. Because the adult is concerned that the child's behavior can embarrass the family, the anger in the adult can reach a level of unhealthiness and the child may suffer greatly for the offense.

"Identify the enemies of your family, not in your family."

Please note this is a difficult topic, but it must be discussed.

I will go on record saying that the confusion and mishandling of punishment that turns into violence towards a child is a direct attack from a belief system that is an enemy to the family. Nothing, absolutely nothing, can be beaten out of a child or an adult. I am only advocating that physical punishing should never be used as a threat or a retaliation type of behavior.

When the adult is angry and operating in self-preservation, physical punishment can easily become a form of violence that is cloaked behind disciplining a child to correct or redirect the poor behavior. Is it possible that this same type of thinking and behavior about punishment is rooted deep into the same mindset of ignorance that all slave masters, dictators, and corrupt leaders operated under, throughout history? I think it is time to decloak this dangerous thinking that produces destructive behavior.

We must now consider the second portion of structure, which is discipline. The oxford dictionary defines **discipline** as the practice of training people to obey rules or a code of behavior, using punishment to correct disobedience.

Discipline is about teaching the person to take ownership and corrective actions towards self as they learn self-control. This process is about what is developing internally. The young person learns about personal character development and the art of saying no to self. The younger the child, the more discipline may be necessary. As a young person grows and develops into more maturity, more self-regulation and self-adjusting should take place. Parents must make room and encourage self-regulation and self-adjusting behaviors.

The third part of structure that a strategic parent must be aware of is consequences. **Consequences** are the results or outcomes of our choices and behaviors. Consequences teach us what works and what does not work in our favor. Therefore, **consequential thinking** means that one can evaluate that there are consequences for my behaviors, both good and bad. Consequential thinking should be more developed at 17 years old than 3 years old.

> **"Young people must be encouraged to exercise their own consequential thinking."**

Let me encourage that parents and young people can greatly benefit from discussions about consequential thinking. **The more conversation is welcome, the less oversight is needed by the parents**. For example, consider how much the parent is continually reminding and checking in about getting homework done.

When parents and youth have discussed and built a healthy understanding of consequences for behavior, the youth will have appropriate thinking and understanding that the completed homework is the youth's responsibility. Young people must be encouraged to exercise their own consequential thinking. Parents are encouraged to make room for this type of growth.

"Discipline is about what develops internally."

Right here it is important to interject the concept of **natural & logical consequences**.

- ❖ A **natural consequence** is not influenced by others; you stand in the rain without an umbrella you will get wet. When we do not take care of personal hygiene, we begin to smell bad, which can draw unwanted comments from others. Parents, please note that this is not the time to be sarcastic and critical. The young person could benefit from your feedback when you say something like: "I have confidence that you will adjust to respond differently next time."

- ❖ **Logical consequence** is more about the person in authority responding to the behavior with reparations that are related, respectful, restorative, responsible and overall helpful. As the authority, what do you really want the offender to learn? Check your motives. An example of a logical consequence: When the young person has not completed an assigned chore, create a monetary deduction for each reminder of chore completion. Limit the reminders to no more than three. The money can be deducted from an allowance or the next fast food run or activity funding. Parents can also consider deducting or limiting data usage on devices as a payment for logical consequence. This includes if someone else volunteers to complete the chore in a timely manner.

"Young people are counting on adults to be easily frustrated, inconsistent and forgetful about things that matter."

The key thing to remember about consequences is: Consistency and Follow-through. **Young people are counting on adults to be easily frustrated, inconsistent and forgetful about things that matter.** When youth have evidence of parents dropping the ball in this category, they deposit it into a lifetime memory bank.

Consider this: Children are real people with real feelings and emotions that want to be seen, heard, and accepted. They may look like a younger version of us, but they are intelligent and beautiful individuals with their own identity and developing view of the world. See them for who they are, not for who we desire or demand them to be!

A strategic parent will develop a healthy structure for the young people in their care. The older children (pre-teens & teenagers) will also benefit by helping parents to develop the structure for the household. Structure and discipline done well can help produce an emotionally healthy young person who can transition into a mentally healthy adult. Though this topic is very taxing, it is also a vital topic that demands a strategic response.

Do not just agree or disagree with the hot topics of this chapter. Please invest the time to evaluate and re-evaluate your family structure when it pertains to punishment, discipline, and consequences. Whatever failures may be present, confess, apologize, forgive, and restore. Love and truth will heal family matters.

"Structure and discipline done well can help produce an emotionally healthy young person who can transition into a mentally healthy adult."

Chapter 5: Knowing Your Position

Parents, the older your child becomes, the more your position, not your title must change. You must move from the person who holds them, scolds them, and protects them, to a position of left or right flank. One definition of flank is "the side of anything, as of a building. The military uses the term to mean the extreme right or left side of the army or fleet.

At the flank position, your view is limited so your trust in your young person must be increased. It is their life. They may not understand the physical and emotional changes that are happening, but they have the firsthand knowledge of what is happening. Also remember, this young person did not come to earth to live your dream or to stay in the shadows of anyone else. We are to position our self to come alongside to support and encourage.

Controlling and dominant parents have major difficulties moving into or accepting a flank position. This difficulty might stem from a thinking process that assigns the parent to the role of expert in the life of the young person. This is sometimes verbalized as: "I know exactly what you are thinking" or "I know everything about you". At the flank position, the strategic parent will not assume ownership or expertise of someone else's life, vision, goals, or directions. Therefore, ask yourself this question: What does the flank position look like for me?

Most of the power struggle issues in the home are happening because parents don't understand the repositioning or will not accept the repositioning. As mentioned before, when the parent is exasperated with a decision or situation and makes this type of comment to that young person, "just forget it, you can just learn the hard way". That is not repositioning to flank, that is the position of abandonment. The parent has physically or emotionally moved to the AWOL position, absent without leave.

Most times this happens because the adult (parent) is not getting their "non-communicated" emotional needs met within the parent—child relationship. Parents have real needs that must be communicated and met. Therefore, parents do not shortchange yourself by continuing to invest in making the world better for a new generation and enduring your own personal suffering. **You are valuable and need support in the journey.** Please do not neglect you.

"Parents are valuable and need support in the journey."

Consider this: What age should the child be when the parent begins **the process of flanking**? The answer to this question depends on the individual. A strategic parent will begin testing out the theory when you desire to see more mature thinking and behaviors from your young person.

A strategic parent will operate from the position of tour guide, not owner or ultimate creator. The role of parenting is temporary because it has a time limit on it. When children grow into adults, who are capable of being responsible for self, they do not require the role of being parented. Accept your position and role freely. The flank position offers the parent a different perspective on the relationship, while also creating room for the young person to experience different aspects of maturity.

The rules of engagement help the strategic parent to become a partner in the relationship with the young person. The adjusted view of the situation for the young person allows them to have a better understanding about life decisions. The flank positioning of the parent creates an opportunity for more dialogue with the young person because trust is now expanded. **Furthermore, the flank position should also add a measure of relief to the parent. Trust what you have invested in your young person.**

"What does the flank position look like for me?

Chapter 6: Hostility and the Hostage

The topic of a power struggle was mentioned in earlier chapters. A power struggle happens when both parties want their own way in any given situation. Power struggles can get violent when either person feels offended by the other person in the conflict. We naturally go into an emotional protection mode of behavior. We are desiring preservation and to win the focus of the conflict.

The focus of this chapter is to help the parent become aware of the power of hostility before, during, or after a conflict. When either the young person or the adult is hostile, they have taken on the characteristics of being unfriendly or antagonistic. Hostility is the fuel for taking someone hostage with anger and disdain for the way that the other person is acting or responding in the moment.

During the hostility of a power struggle, the parent might have to become the hostage negotiator of the situation. The key to negotiation during hostility is to locate the origin of the issue. There is no quick fix in dealing with hostility. We each must admit when we are upset and not thinking clearly in the moment, before the hostile act becomes full blown anger with repercussions.

Consider this: All members of the family must learn the power of hostility. Parents must teach the principle that all hostile moves, thoughts, and behaviors are processes designed to take someone hostage in any situation. Therefore, we must check our hostility by identifying how we are thinking and feeling about our desires.

Responsibility and accountability are powerful resources to help deal with this behavior. *A strategic parent is always evaluating what forces are enemies to the family.*

"Hostility is the fuel for taking someone hostage with anger and disdain."

Chapter 7: Principles of the House

What are the principles of your home? What do you see as valuable? What do your children see as valuable? This is not about items that money can buy or manipulate. This is about depth of character and belief. Every individual is welcome to have their own belief system and understanding of some type of higher power or deity. With this higher power or deity is the acceptance and belief in something bigger than self.

Choose who and what you will believe and speak freely to your family about those beliefs. From that belief, create or adopt some non-negotiable principles for your home. These principles can change the focus and direction of family conversations and relationships. Find what works for you. Here are four that I have adopted and value:

> ➤ "Do not judge others, and you will not be judged. For you will be treated as you treat others. The standard you use in judging is the standard by which you will be judged" (Matthew 7:1-2 NLT).
> ➤ "Know well the condition of your flocks and give attention to your herds" (Proverbs 27:23 ESV).
> ➤ "Love is patient and kind. Love is not jealous or boastful or proud or rude. It does not demand its own way. It is not irritable, and it keeps no record of being wrong. It does not rejoice about injustice but rejoices whenever the truth wins out. Love never gives up, never loses faith, is always hopeful, and endures through every circumstance" (1 Corinthians 13:4-7 NLT).
> ➤ *"You don't miss the water until the well runs dry."* – Wise words from my grandmother, Ida Mae Johnson.

Each of the principles above are loaded with nuggets of helpful thoughts and ideas that challenge the behavior of every family member. The principles support the development of character and create an atmosphere for healthy conversations with young people. If you just leave it to chance, be assured others will gladly come in to influence how your children think. The influence has already begun.

"A Change in Strategy can change your world." From Tim Timberlake

*The next chapter of this book is not in the table of contents. The chapter is strategically placed and named. The chapter is called **Silence**. True silence is learning to be still. The importance of being still helps us to digest the issues of life. We take this behavior for granted by either not using it or pretending that we get this when we are sleeping. So, I encourage you to spend the next 15 – 45 minutes in silent stillness without created noise or sleep. Just you and your thoughts. Try to silence your thoughts as well. Allow your mind to remain focused on the word silence so that you are more likely to complete the action. My desire is that you will allow silence to arrest you with the joy of just relaxing your thoughts and concerns. It's okay as a parent to just be still.*

Silence

"Silence is not our enemy."

Chapter 8: Maturity is a privilege

Age is not the owner of maturity. Getting older will not transform you into a mature person. Maturity is a privilege and not a right. Maturity is the offspring of wisdom. Wisdom challenges our thoughts and actions. My actions are directly related to my thinking. How you think is how you act. Wisdom happens in my mind and then my actions follow along.

Everyone should ask themselves: what does maturity look like on me? Maturity will make us do things that immaturity would not even notice. When my thoughts change, my actions will follow. I see many parents and adults completely disappointed in the actions of their children and students. The adult might even say, "I'm really mad or disappointed in your behavior".

Let us consider saying this instead: "It appears that your thinking is causing you to act in ways that are disappointing". The second statement places the burden of responsibility on the young person without the adult becoming the focus of the scenario. Furthermore, the second response reinforces the concept of *thinking controls behavior*. When our thinking improves, our behaviors will follow suit.

We encourage parents and adults to stop focusing on correcting the actions and teach the young person to identify the thinking that feeds those actions. Each person must identify the problem and want to change the thinking. When the young person identifies their own character flaws, due to incorrect thinking, they can self-correct, which is a great sign of maturity. This type of metamorphosis requires guidance and space to develop emotionally without the hovering, controlling, or impatient parenting that we can all fall into.

The strategic parent will make room for the maturity of the young person. This type of parenting is looking for signs of maturity instead of focusing all energies on calling out behaviors that do not fit the style of the parents' upbringing.

Consider this: The parenting of the 21st century requires a different approach that is not repetitious of "the good old days". We cannot place new wine in old wine skins. Remember, we are raising young people who are leading in the future, not the past.

Your young person is becoming who they will be in the future, right now. Parents have a great opportunity to adjust their thinking to a more strategic method of engaging with the young people of this era. This new generation requires an upgrade in parenting.

"When my thoughts change, my actions will follow."

Chapter 9: Asking Questions

The best resource for learning firsthand information is to ask questions. What is your favorite color? What happened today that caused you to feel hurt or discouraged? How many hours did you spend playing video games this week? When asking questions, it is easy to sound as if you are interrogating your child. Let me encourage your technique and strategy with this statement: **Ask questions for the purpose of getting to know them and how they function instead of asking questions with the motive of fixing them or the situation they are in.** We cannot be the fixer of everything. Wreck-it-Ralph® and Fix-it Felix® are cartoon characters from a game, not methods of interacting within the family.

Parents, as your young person is transitioning to adulthood, guard yourself from continually going to the

9-1-1 dispatch position of seeing everything as an emergency. Young people will remind us "it's not that big of a deal"—and most times they are correct with this evaluation. Young people must be encouraged and expected to identify their own resolutions to their own problems—this builds maturity.

Asking the right questions:

Let me say that I think that young people are awesome with their not fully developed brains. Human Anatomy & Physiology teaches us that the frontal lobe, which is the decision controls of the human brain, is not fully developed until the mid to late 20's.

For years, I have worked with and around youth who have some form of crisis behaviors that involve law enforcement or the legal system. When I meet them and interact with them, I will have to ask different questions in order to gain my own perspective of the situation. I will lead with an open-ended question like: Tell me what happened that caused the police to be called to the situation? After the question, I listen with the intent of **hearing their story**. If a parent is present during my questions, they might respond to the child's comments with: "well, you didn't say any of that earlier" and the young person will reply with **"no one ever asked"**.

Sometimes the reason that "no one ever asked" is because the adult or adults on the scene of the "crime" or behavior have already prejudged and condemned the youth. Therefore, they approach the young person with an attitude of distrust and ridicule, which will limit what questions and conclusions that will be offered.

"No one ever asked"…

Dear Parents, asking the right questions and choosing to **listen with the intent of hearing their experience**, without judgment, condemnation, or advice can create a powerful connection and strengthen the core of your relationship.

An additional aspect to the right question is asking more open-ended questions instead of mostly closed-ended questions. Let me define the specifics of this process. A closed-ended question produces short, factual answers or in some cases a sound effect of compliance. An open-ended question can produce a longer answer or a better view of the big picture. Open-ended questions are used to invite more dialogue than just a simple one word or short phrase reply. Whereas, close-ended questions produce short answers, that are sometimes factual answers.

A common, and overused closed-ended question that children are regularly asked is: how was school today? Most parents, especially our beautiful moms, desire a play by play account of the school day events. Children will often give the common response: "fine" or "it was okay". A strategic parent will use the new understanding about asking questions that create more dialogue.

Check out these examples:

Close-ended:

- What is your address?
- Do you have values?
- How was school today?

Open-ended:

- What was it like growing up in your neighborhood?
- Tell me about your values?
- Tell me something about your school day that you do not mind sharing?

The open-ended question will create an atmosphere to learn more about the experience. Each phrase or comment of their answer can also be converted into a next level question by the parent saying: "Tell me more about that". Remember this is not about interrogation, it's about validation of an experience from the perspective of the storyteller. Two people at the same location and time will have their own individual story about that same experience.

Consider this: The strategic parent will learn the art of asking better questions that create healthy dialogue within the family. The technique of asking questions cannot be a type of interrogation. And remember that the motivation is for creating relationship with your young person. Just as you may ask questions, invite your family members to also ask you questions. A strategic parent will teach what they have learned.

"Create an atmosphere to learn more about the experience from the perspective of the storyteller."

Chapter 10: Grow My Character

Ask yourself and your child:

What is self-discipline? How do I demonstrate loyalty? What does it mean to build a healthy friendship? We live in a time when many voices are speaking to our children about who they should be and how they should look, live, and love. What's your opinion mom, dad, grandparents and relatives? The squeaky wheel still gets the oil, therefore, make some noise.

Young people still need parents and helpful adults who care more about their character development, than their social following. (This does not mean that parents should not be aware of the social platforms of their children). A strategic parent will teach young people about perseverance and determination. ***Quality character is not***

inherited, it is developed. The sooner they learn good character traits, the more they will practice and develop those traits. The thoughts and actions of quality traits will influence the depth of wisdom. That wisdom communicates and demonstrates maturity. Therefore, invest in character development before someone with wrong motives comes into your territory.

Honesty and integrity do not come naturally, we are born liars. When I was a little girl, I was a thief. If I wanted something, I felt I had to take it for myself. I didn't just grow out of it, I needed healthy adults to teach me about self-respect and gratitude. This helped me to understand that stealing was wrong behavior. Strategic parents must evaluate who has permission to teach your young people about quality character.

Talk to your youth about handling disappointment before the major disappointments happen. Create discussions about values and do not assume that they will adopt your personal values. And remember, while you are teaching them, let them teach you.

Consider this: The strategic parent will recognize that young people are valuable resources for seeing the world through their own eyes. Only the young person can communicate what they are seeing and experiencing. Show them respect, honor and appreciation for that expression and communication. This requires no assumptions, no comparisons, no condemnations, and no judgment. For some adults, this might be a major challenge, but the relational results will be priceless.

"Invest in Character Development."

Chapter 11: Does it have to be FAIR?

The County Fair is my favorite place to get cotton candy, kettle corn, funnel cakes and the greasy corn dogs! Oh, were we not talking about favorite fattening foods of all time? My apologies (LOL). We have all heard it and we have all probably said it: "that's not fair". So, who let the fairness police into the conversation? And who taught children to use this phrase as a comeback remark of disappointment and dismissal of adult decisions? **These are important questions, but the key point is—the questioning concept of fairness is fair.** When parents make decisions and decrees, some form of measurement must be used.

Here's something to ponder in this dilemma: Consider

countering the fairness challenge with balance. I propose that our human nature is truly seeking **BALANCE Over Fairness**. The advantage of balance over fairness is a fine line of understanding that fairness demands equality (mainly based on the one making the demands) and balance requires equity. **Equity** in relationships is simply taking the time to acknowledge that everyone has a story and desires that their story be heard. Therefore, balance invites us to listen.

Dear Parents, let me encourage you to use balance as your measuring tool for decisions about discipline and consequences. We do not always get it right, but we must always get involved. True balance requires going beyond the initial reaction to the circumstances and behaviors.

Anytime someone has stated "that's not fair", it is a great time to investigate their meaning of fairness. The meaning will usually have something to do with one of the most disliked subjects of our existence—the subject of math.

The person claiming the unfairness is seeking a solution that is either greater than, less than, or equal. The parent can speak to the true need and desire for balance. When things are out of balance, we feel unstable, insecure, and fearful. These ingredients are powerful and cause reasons to have conflict with the other person who is opposing them.

"Fairness demands equality. Balance requires equity."

As we continue to ponder fairness, here are some further thoughts: The word justification is engrafted in the human DNA, which I believe originated from the Creator God. Which might have something to do with why we love television programs that tell stories with the same legal issues that require justice being served.

Humans desire justice because of a Just God. These same humans have watered down the holiness of justice to a weaker concept of fairness. True justification means only the righteous judge can decide. Therefore, none of us can attain to that role, so we fight for justice, fairness, and equality at one level or another.

Consider this: Why is the fairness complaint looked upon with dismissal and negativity by the adults? The evaluation of unfairness is about being insightful and aware. This phrase creates a great opportunity for healthy discussion between a parent and young person. Please take full advantage of this opportunity.

In summation, a strategic parent will engage the young person in the discussion of fairness. Ask your young person about their definition of fairness. Ask your young person to explain what they feel needs to be balanced in the situation. Validate your young person for their correct evaluation of the situation. Your validation and engagement will reduce and remove the power struggle or verbal conflict that can ensue.

"The question of fairness is fair."

Chapter 12: The Village

Most of us have heard the statement: *"It takes a village to raise a child"*. This statement is often spoken, though it does have some question as to its origin and purpose. It is often spoken in support or defense of communities banding together to help the children in poverty based on socioeconomic issues, political dynamics, or educational exposure conditions. These items have their own merit and positional priority for each community, but this chapter will seek to focus in on the statement as a question. Does it really take a village to raise a child?

The first step in the quest to answer this statement of curiosity is to determine who makes up the village. Well, since this is my project, in my village there are teachers, other family members, some church people, some community leaders from local government, local stores, and a few of my neighbors. Now that I have constructed my own specific village, the second step is to decide where do I, as the parent, fit into the village? And furthermore, where does my child fit in this village? Now, this rabbit trail of questions can lead to even more questions about the rights, roles, and responsibilities of the village people. But, for the sake of time and confusion, let us stay focused on the main question: does it take a village to raise a child?

Let us just fast forward to the good stuff that identifies the village as a group of busy bodies who think they know more about your child than you do. Sometimes the village is self-promoting by wanting other communities to see what they have done for the wretched children who would not make it in the world if it was not for the wonderful help of a village person or people. There are some village people who are "leaders" and they just usurp the authority of the parent and start demanding that the child be raised a certain way. If you defy that village leader (who might also be an idiot) you are cast out or banished from the "village". I could go on with discussing the role of the expert, the global perspective on child-rearing, or the faithfully inconsistent absentee parent scenarios. But the question remains: Does it take a village to raise a child? No!

It does not take a village to raise a child, but the right village people can help support the parental process. We need each other. Parents need support. Children need support. Parents and children need breaks from each other. But generic, self-serving, self-righteous individuals who become contributors to the problem and not contributors of the solution, should not be welcome to your village gathering party.

It would be nice if we could send out applications requesting quality village people as we prepare to welcome this new child into the world. A quality candidate for a village person sees both the parent and the child as valuable, important people. They are non-judgmental of the parental dynamics and have no problem yielding to support the true need of the family as communicated by the parents, instead of trying to dictate the need of the family.

Therefore, having the right village people in the village that influences the parent and child for the good of family unity is an asset. Be cautious of the village idiot, they might be a wolf in sheep's clothing coming to destroy the process of growing a successful family. All of this is being said so that we examine a new perspective on the "village" of the 21st century. The right village people are required for a productive village environment.

Consider this: You, as a strategic parent, are the CEO of your family. Treat all the family members as important and valuable. The village can be either supportive and helpful or divisive, belittling, and controlling. You set the tone for how others are involved with your family, therefore, be aware. **Never allow the village to become more important than the family.**

"The right village people can help support the family vision."

Conclusion

Throughout this book, there has been a continuing thread of enticement for the reader to consider whom or what is the enemy of the family. The strategic parent must be engaged and aware in order to defend the home and family. Enemies come in all shapes, forms, and sizes.

Some of the parenting and interactions of adults that is happening in this new century is operating as if the children are the enemy. We may not say this out loud, but our thoughts, responses, and actions are saying otherwise. The verbal and emotional attacks on children and young people are heavily destructive and will cripple the leaders of the next generation.

There is an enemy (and multiple enemies), but each family is responsible for identifying the source and entity on their own. The purpose and focus of this resource, is to encourage parents and adults, who interact with children and youth, to examine their methods of operation. We desire that parents adopt an upgrade to strategic parenting to build healthier relationships with the young people in your care.

The family is made of individuals who each have a role and position to play in the family unit. Children are not lesser humans who only become valuable in this world when they are contributing adults. Children are valuable assets to humanity. The rules of engagement amplify that if I focus my energies and resources on the wrong entity or idea, my family will suffer significant loss. When the family suffers, the world suffers. Family is our greatest resource; therefore, may we be strategic as we parent and engage the next generation of leaders.

Thank you to our parents and adults who work with young people at every level. You are valuable and needed in this journey for developing great leaders for the future. Be aware of your role, positioning, and rules of engagement and the value of your influence.

"When the family suffers, the world suffers."

Bonus Material: Questions & Notes

Here are a few *Pause & Ponder* questions for the reader to consider and interact. You are welcome to send your questions and comments to the author at info@themadiselgroup.com :

What are your priorities for the parent-child relationship?

After reading the book, what are your views on the topic of respect and how do they differ from the author or your child?

What are your hopes and desires for your child's future and how will you support their journey?

Name and discuss two family events that have made a lasting impression on you and your children?

What are the top five-character traits that every parent should teach children by the age of 13? (Please also explain the importance)

What key principles did you gain from this resource and how will those principles make a difference in your interactions with children, family, friends, and co-workers?

Notes

<u>Notes</u>

MORE INFORMATION ABOUT THE AUTHOR

Sandra D. Johnson is the founder and CEO of The Madisel Group, LLC. The Madisel Group is a collective of Life Coaches and Consultants that range in services in lifestyle management, financial matters, marriage and relationships, as well as youth & family dynamics. The focus of each of these areas is for personal and emotional wellness of every individual.

For more information about us, go to www.themadiselgroup.com and also connect with us on social media and podcast on @MadiselCoach. Please also send for more information about this project and other future projects to info@themadiselgroup.com

Made in the USA
Columbia, SC
03 November 2019

82490184R00057